BOSTON SOCIAL SCIENCE ASSOCIATION.

CHEAP FOOD

DEPENDENT ON

CHEAP TRANSPORTATION:

AN ADDRESS

DELIVERED BEFORE THE

BOSTON SOCIAL SCIENCE ASSOCIATION,

JANUARY, 14th, 1869,

BY

JOSIAH QUINCY,

ITS PRESIDENT.

BOSTON:
1869.
J. H. EASTBURN'S PRESS.

CHEAP FOOD DEPENDENT ON CHEAP TRANSPORTATION.

I have been requested, by your Committee, to prepare a paper on the causes of the present high prices of food.

It is a subject intimately connected with the comfort of the individual and the strength of the nation. If plain nourishing food is made inaccessible to the poor, and diminished in quantity for a large portion of the community, as is the case at present, it is an evil that strikes vitally at the best interests of society.

The causes of the variation of prices are traced, in the exhaustive statements of THOMAS TOOKE, contained in six octavo volumes. First, to alterations in the value of the currency: Secondly, to war, with its attendant taxes: Thirdly, to varieties in the seasons.

Under the first head, he discusses the depreciation of money— or the diminished value of the precious metals in the commercial world —also the depreciation of the currency which becomes of less value than the coin it promises to pay. There follows a full comparison of prices from 1797, when specie payment was suspended by the Bank of England, to its resumption in 1823; proving that there was no progressive rise in the prices of necessaries, and the wages of labor, during the period of the bank restriction — that corn was as low in the summer of 1804, and meat in 1808, as it had been in 1798, and many descriptions of labor were lower in 1811 than in 1797, and concluding therefrom that the utmost effect of the bank restriction on prices may be measured by the average excess of the market price above the price of gold. In estimating the degree to which war, or a transition from war to peace, may affect general prices, two questions arise:

1st. How far taxes, requisite to pay extraordinary expenses, are calculated to raise prices;

2nd. In what degree, independent of that in which they may be affected by taxation, are the necessaries of life influenced by war, and in what degree through the medium of supply and demand? Taxes on particular commodities raise their price, and if manufactured, the prices of the raw materials, but it does not follow that all other articles, if untaxed, should be raised in price, and the operation of taxes is therefore excluded from among the causes of the fluctuation in the prices of untaxed commodities, such as agricultural products, or of commodities divested of taxes to which they may be liable on importation or consumption.

In reply to the argument that an extra demand or consumption arises from a state of war, Mr. Tooke argues that except for naval and military stores, there is no necessity for an advance of price, as the expenditure by Government on necessaries is exactly what would have been laid out by individuals upon objects of consumption, productive or unproductive. This would be the case if war supplies for the year were raised by direct taxation. The same result is obtained if the Government borrow; the money advanced to the Government would, but for the loan, have been laid out equally in purchases. It is precisely like money lent on mortgage to individuals, the lender would have just so much less, and the borrower so much more to lay out. It follows that the extra demand, arising from Government expenditure, cannot have the effect of raising the aggregate of prices, and this is fully borne out by the facts stated.

Two of the causes mentioned by Mr. Tooke need not be considered. Our war has passed but the taxes remain, and of course enhance the prices of all articles that are subject to them. Money has been depreciated by the immense additions to the amount of gold drawn from California and Australia, and still more by the compulsory substitution of greenbacks. But it is not the nominal value of the circulating medium that makes cheap or dear necessaries of life; cheapness depends on the fertility of the seasons and the surplus that remains of previous crops, and above all, *on the facilities of transportation.* All interested in agricultural produce are alive to the prodigious influence of the weather, at particular periods, on the result of the harvest in quantity or in exchangeable value. Mr. Tooke thinks that variations in price arise chiefly from this source.

In discussing the effect produced by quantity on price, he proves that a small deficiency in produce, compared with the average consumption, causes a rise very much beyond the ratio of defect — that one-tenth defect causes a rise of three-tenths — that when corn rises to treble the common rate, it may be presumed we want above one-third of the common produce — and that if we want five-tenths or one-half the common produce the price would rise to near five times the common rate. No such strict rule can be deduced, but there have been repeated instances, where corn rose from one hundred to two hundred per cent., where the deficiency has not been more than between one-third or one-sixth of an average. The result of this law is very curious. When the crop in England was thirty-two millions of quarters its average price was forty shillings, or £64,000,000 — when it was twenty-eight millions of quarters the price was sixty shillings a quarter, or £84,000,000. The larger quantity being worth £20,000,000 less than the smaller. The great prosperity of the agricultural interest, as it arose from scarcity, was attended with great suffering to the rest of the community, while the return of abundance, which is productive, during the decline of prices, of great distress to that body, is attended with great increase of enjoyment and of real wealth to the rest of the community.

In applying the views of the author I have referred to, we must remember the changes that have taken place, affecting the price and value of almost every article of necessary consumption. At the time of the Revolution, civilization had advanced but a short distance beyond Albany, and had not reached Pittsburgh. The farmer in the country subsisted on what he could raise, and the clothing of the family was spun and woven at home. He required money enough to pay taxes, and what else he wanted was obtained by barter at the village store. There was but one public granary in New England, which stood where Park Street Church now stands, and here the Selectmen annually placed the enormous quantity of twelve thousand bushels of corn, to guard the people from the extravagant prices of speculators. The food required for a population of less than twenty thousand inhabitants, was drawn from the immediate neighborhood, or when the sleighing was good, from an hundred or two miles from the interior. In process of time, emigration and civilization advanced, and the people of New England found that a division of labor rendered it profitable for them to pursue manufactures, commerce, and the fisheries, and depend on the more fertile fields of western New York and

Ohio, for their food. Most of us can remember when Genessee flour stood first in the market. It is heard of no more. The soil has been exhausted by improvident cropping, the yield is small, the quality poor, and the Granary of New England has been removed farther west. Prices depend on demand and supply. The population of Boston has increased ten fold — the agricultural product of the State, in cereals, not at all. The farmers' sons instead of following the plough, are measuring ribbons, and speculating in stocks, or have emigrated to the West — and the farmers' daughters, instead of attending to the dairy are following the spinning jenny, or practising on the piano, and too much of the hard labor is performed by emigrants, who have become almost a necessity of our existence.

Many persons believe that the prices of meat, corn, and wheat, are influenced by speculations on a large scale, in Chicago, and other western cities, and in a smaller degree in our own markets.

Let us consider, for a moment, the resources, and the modes of doing business at one of the great centres of the provision trade. To begin with the meat market in Chicago — according to Mr. PARTON, three hundred thousand cattle, one-third of the three millions of hogs, packed at the West, and sheep and calves without number, are received, lodged, entertained, and dispatched, every year, from this market alone. They are sold to dealers who transport them directly by railroad to Albany, and thence to New York and Boston. The price is governed by demand and supply. This is a kind of stock that cannot be held, for the fat animal might eat his own value while waiting for a market.

But it is then said, it is forestallers in our own market — that the butchers in Faneuil Hall Market regulate the price to suit themselves. But here again it is supply and demand.

It is amusing to look back on the action of our ancestors, who being ignorant of the first principles of Political Economy, charged the price of meat first to the market houses — and a mob pulled them down — then to the butchers, and to spite them, in 1778, they passed a resolution to eat fish two days in the week. The result was, that supply and demand again interfered — the price of fish rose — so they abused the fishmongers, and went back to the butchers for protection.

The arrangements of our Market are as perfect as can be devised. By the very able report of the Committee on Free Markets, (Document 100, of 1865,) it appears that there were then seven hundred and thirty-nine Provision Stores in the city — that persons may occupy Street Stands free, for sale of produce of their own farm, or of any person residing within ten miles of them — or may go about from house to house selling fruit and provision — that only about five hundred families depend on Faneuil Hall Market, and that the rent of the stalls would not add more than one-tenth of a cent to a piece of beef weighing thirty pounds. The perusal of the above mentioned report must convince any reader that the prices are not unduly influenced by any combination in the Market.

The immense quantity of grain raised at the West, must prevent any speculation based on obtaining a monopoly, or even a control of the market. Four years ago, the exports from Chicago alone amounted to over fifty-three millions of bushels in the berry, and three millions of barrels of flour. There are many other western markets that fall but little behind, and besides these, the rich farmers hold millions of bushels for a price, which would, on a sufficient rise, be thrown at once upon the market, and defeat any permanent success of a speculation.

In considering the supply of food for New England, two elements must be taken into view.—The fertility of the season, and the facility of transportation.—The diminution of production, and the impediments to communication. The effect of the latter is to produce a glut of the exportable, and a dearth of the importable.

Hemp was at the same price in Russia, in the years 1809, during the dynasty of NAPOLEON, and in 1823, after his overthrow, and yet, in the former year, it was worth in the London market thirty pounds, and in the latter, three — and the same effect was seen during the late rebellion at the South — Cotton was very valuable in Liverpool, and a perfect drug in Charleston. The national blockade made all the difference in prices at the two points. It was upon this matter of transportation that the rebels relied for the intervention of England and France. They believed, as the secessionists told Mr. RUSSELL, at the Charleston Club, just after the attack on Fort Sumter,— "We know John Bull very well,—he will make a great fuss about non-interference at first, but when he begins to want cotton, he will come off his perch. We have only to shut off your supply for a few weeks, and we can create a revolution in Great Britain. There are four millions of your people depending upon us, for bread."

Situated as we are, prices of necessaries depend eminently on transportation. The price of the bullock that is raised in Brighton is the same as the cost of the bullock raised in Texas, with transportation added. Now our railroad managers find it difficult to find what it costs to run a train a mile. We must therefore go to England for statistics, and ask those who are not satisfied, to tell us the difference in cost, and its cause.

According to the report of the English Board of Trade, for 1863, the average expenditure per train per mile, taking all the railways in the United Kingdom, was two shillings and sixpence, or sixty-three cents in gold. This statement is made with the understanding that the ordinary current expenses of the railroad are paid, and that the tracks, engines, wagons, carriages, etc., are kept in efficient repair, and replaced whenever necessary. Over the level roads of the West a train can probably move three hundred tons. Two hundred tons can, with a little assistance at the Summit, be carried from Albany to Boston, by a single engine. At the English estimate, calling it one thousand miles from Chicago to Boston, it would cost six hundred and thirty dollars to bring two hundred tons. The railroads would be kept up, but no dividends would be made on the stock. Let us look at the margin that would be left for profit on such a basis. The trains from the West generally running full, and those from the East, at least, paying their expenses.

Calling it but two thousand pounds to the ton, what is the result?

Freight of corn, from Chicago, is 85 cents per 100 lbs., or $17 a ton.

A train carrying two hundred tons would give . .	$3,400
Cost of train, as by English estimate, ...	630
For dividends on each train, ...	$2,770

A barrel of flour weighs, on an average, two hundred lbs., or ten to a ton, freight $1.60, or $16 a ton.

Or for a train of two hundred tons, ...	$3,200
Cost as above, ...	630
For dividends on each train, ...	$2,570

Beef and pork, six barrels to the ton, at $3 per bbl., or $18 a ton.

Two hundred tons, ...	$3,600
Deduct, ...	630
For dividends, ...	$2,970

This estimate of cost is singularly corroborated by what Mr. GALT tells us is the only case in which the manager of a railroad ever entered into minute details showing the actual cost of conveying coal. The details are given in a paper which I read in 1866, before the Board of Trade, and which the Common Council of this city did me honor to reprint as one of their documents, No. 109.

The result is that it cost one shilling and fourpence, or thirty-two cents, to carry a ton of coal one hundred miles, or three dollars and twenty cents for a thousand, or six hundred and forty dollars for a train carrying two hundred tons for that distance.

There may be differences between the cost of transportation in England and the United States. But if you double the cost, in America, the profits, by the foregoing estimates, amount, on an average, to two thousand dollars to a train, which accounts for Mr. VANDERBILT'S assumption that the receipts of the New York Central, over and above the dividends, have amounted to the enormous sum of twenty-two million, eight hundred and twenty-nine thousand, six hundred dollars.

But no such satisfactory results as to cost, can be obtained. Our railroad reports to the Legislature are, in the language of one of the Presidents, "made up arbitrarily the best way we can."

Mr. GALT in his admirable work on "Railway Reform," after showing from actual experiment that railroads in England had carried passengers at low rates, without affecting dividends, concludes by saying, "When the public come to know that a passenger

2

can be conveyed one hundred miles for two pence half-penny, (or five cents) for which he is charged eight shillings and fourpence, (or two dollars) and a ton can be brought from the North of England for about a shilling, (or twenty-four cents) the cost there being six or seven shillings, and the price in London four or five times that sum, it requires no prophet to foretell that the days of railway monopoly, in private hands, will soon in this country (England) be numbered." The railways in Ireland will soon be purchased by the government, and they will be in America, as soon as the people can understand the amount of taxes imposed on their daily bread by monopolies.

The question of primary importance, is upon what proportion of property represented by a corporation shall dividends be paid? Shall it be on all moneys expended on the road, whether furnished by the shareholders, the public or the government? Or upon the amount only of such expenditure actually contributed by the shareholders? If the people, through their representatives, have made a grant of land sufficient to pay for one-half of the road, is it just that they shall pay interest forever on the whole, notwithstanding their contribution?

A writer in the New York *Evening Post*, of January 15th, states, "That not less than ten great States, each of them larger than New York, each of them sure to contain, within a century, not less than five millions of people, have been given over to the control of these irresponsible monopolies. All of them were obtained by the projectors without the investment of a dollar of their own, except in lobbying."

Should the people, after such a contribution, be compelled forever to pay dividends on the *whole cost* of a road to those who have contributed little or nothing in cash to its construction?

Again it is said that the issue of unpaid stock is made to represent the surplus earnings of the road, invested in construction, over and above the regular dividends made to the shareholders. Now how has that surplus been acquired? Manifestly from the high fares imposed upon the patrons of the road. So that in reality, the people who have paid, by this surplus, for the construction of the road, are obliged also to pay interest upon the money they themselves have paid for the benefit of the corporation, if it is entitled to dividends on the whole increased value of the road.

Should this view be approved by the legislators, they can easily find out from the books of the corporation, or from the testimony of any original stockholder the amount that has been paid in as cash by the shareholders. And then forbid any director, under severe penalities, from making any dividends on a greater amount than the sum so paid, disregarding the number of shares into which the stock of the corporation may have been divided. Would not such a course do justice to those who have in fact paid for their proportion of the road, and cause great reductions to be made in the cost of transportation.

A few facts will elucidate my position.

On Saturday, the 19th of December last, after the close of business hours, the Directors of the New York Central Railroad declared a scrip dividend, from net earnings applied to construction, equal to eighty per cent., upon a share capital of $28,537,000. The amount of the scrip dividend is $22,829,600. Upon both stock and scrip a semi-annual cash dividend of four per cent. The total dividends consequently equal eighty-eight per cent. on the present share capital of fifty-one million, three hundred and sixty-seven thousand, six hundred dollars, ($51,367,600.)

A writer in the New York *Evening Post*, shows, from the sworn returns of the managers, that none, or comparatively a very small amount, of net earnings have ever been applied, as alleged, to construction.

After the consolidation of the road in 1853, a scrip or sham dividend, equalling $8,894,500 of estimated values over cost, was made to the stockholders. Upon this sum the public have since that time been paying interest.

A similar dividend, equalling	$22,829,600
is now paid, the two together amount to	31,724,100
The interest on this sum, at eight per cent., is . . .	2,537,928

Two million, five hundred and thirty-seven thousand, nine hundred and twenty-eight dollars.

This enormous sum measures the tax which the managers of the Central Railroad have imposed annually for all time, upon the commercial and travelling community, and for which not a single penny of equivalent has been or will be returned.

The amount of unpaid stock between Chicago and Boston, as given in the admirable Essay of CHARLES FRANCIS ADAMS, Jr., in the last *North American Review*, on "Railroad inflation," is—

Between Boston and Albany, ...	$2,000,000
On the New York Central, ...	31,724,100
Between Erie and Buffalo, ...	2,200,000
Between Erie and Cleveland, ...	6,181,573
Between Cleveland and Chicago, ...	3,000,000
	$45,105,673

That is to say, that on this line between Boston and Chicago, the people are taxed between four and five million of dollars annually, to pay dividends on over forty-five million of stock that never cost its holders a cent.

Mr. VANDERBILT'S justification for this issue of stock, as I gather it from his testimony before Judge INGRAHAM, amounts to this: That by high charges, the corporation has taken the money of the people and expended it on the road, and that therefore it has a right to charge the people forever, with dividend on the twenty-two million, eight hundred and twenty-nine thousand, six hundred dollars, which they have already paid. The feudal Barons on the Rhine, those transportation managers during the dark ages, compelled all that passed to pay tribute; but they lacked the master-stroke of "financeering," in neglecting to compel the people to pay interest forever on the very sums of which they had been plundered.

Attempts have been made to introduce New York customs into Massachusetts, in one case on a steam railroad unsuccessfully, and in the other with temporary apparent success.

The Managers of the Hartford and New Haven Railroad, and of the New York and New Haven Railroads, proposed to obtain from the State of Connecticut authority to consolidate the two, and to issue shares to an amount equal to the market value of their stock, the former being worth two hundred and the latter one hundred and forty. Thus giving, without requiring a cent in payment, three million of dollars to the shareholders of the Hartford and New Haven, and two million four hundred thousand to those of the New York and New Haven, and imposing a tax for the benefit of these shareholders, of more than half a million of dollars per annum forever, on all business passing by railroad up the valley of the Connecticut. The object was fortunately discovered in the Legislature of last winter, and that it could be defeated by simply repealing a line in the statute of 1852, that authorized such a connection. This was done, and the bill vetoed by the Governor; and then, an old member told me, a scene occurred unlike any one he had ever before witnessed. Millions of dollars were depending! All the lobby members were retained and influential lawyers feed, but the members had been made to understand their duty, and it was in vain. The representatives were true to the people, and the bill passed over the veto of the Governor by seventeen to four in the Senate, and by one hundred and fifty-five to thirty-four in the House.

This scheme was thus happily, for the interests of the public, defeated. There is on record, another similar enterprise, undertaken nearer home, which up to the present time, has been apparently successful. In 1866, the Legislature of Massachussetts, at the instance of the Directors of the Western Railroad, granted an increase of capital for the purpose of completing and equipping the road. We will refer at once to official documents.

In reply to a call from the legislature, Mr. CHARLES E. STEVENS, Treasurer of the Western and of the Boston and Albany Railroad, stated that (in Document No. 98, House of Representatives,) "The Western Railroad Corporation has issued during the past year, twenty thousand one hundred and forty-three shares of stock, one hundred and forty-three of which were issued, in conformity with a vote of the previous year, for cash, and the proceeds formed a part of the funds expended for construction during the year.

"The twenty thousand shares were issued to represent moneys that had been borrowed and expended in constructing and equipping the Hudson and Berkshire, now Hudson and Boston road, the Albany and West Stockbridge, and the Western roads. This sum, namely, $2,000-000, was charged to the accumulated earnings of the sinking fund.

The issue of stock by the Western Railroad Corporation was made under authority of Chapter 300 of the acts of the year 1866."

The portion of this act applicable to this question, is as follows:

By Section 1, the Western Railroad was authorized to increase its capital stock $3,800,000, — of this, $1,850,000 was appropriated to the construction of the bridge over the Hudson, and the completion of the double track, and the necessary equipment of the road, and not more than eighteen thousand five hundred shares should be issued before the first of January, 1867.

The second section is in these words:

"Before any sale of the new shares authorized to be created by this act, the Directors of said Corporation shall give notice in writing, of such authorized increase to the Treasurer of the Commonwealth and to the other stockholders, and within thirty days after such notice, the Commonwealth and other stockholders may take, at the par value thereof, their proportion of such increased shares, according to the number of shares in such capital stock owned by them severally at the date of such increase. And if any shares then remain unsold, the said Corporation may dispose of the same at not less than the par value thereof.

"Section 3d. When notice of any such increase of capital stock shall be given to the Treasurer of the Commonwealth, the Governor with the advice and consent of the Council, is hereby authorized to instruct the Treasurer to take the proportion of shares, to which the Commonwealth may be entitled, or any part thereof, and the Governor with the advice and consent of the Council, may draw his warrant on the Treasurer in payment thereof, and such temporary loans are hereby authorized to be obtained by the Treasurer as may be necessary for the payment of the amount thus drawn for."

The phraseology of the act is almost identical with those which had granted the previous issues of stock. In authorizing, therefore, the issue of unpaid stock, it was necessary for the directors to assume, that the language of the statute respecting "sales of the shares," authorizing the stockholders to take shares at par, forbidding the company to sell any remaining shares at less than par value, also the provisions for borrowing money to pay the assessment of the State, had no meaning, or none at least which railroad directors were bound to respect. And in face of the plain prohibitory language of the act, they assumed the power to issue stock, not to be paid for at all, but to remain a tax on the people of Massachusetts forever, for the benefit of the shareholders of the Corporation. On the second day of January, 1867, previous to this issue, the Directors signed a report to the stockholders, containing these words: "This increase was asked for by the corporation, in order to provide funds for the completion of the second track, to make such other additions to the facilities of the road as the increasing business should render necessary, and to purchase, as opportunity may offer, any of the outstanding obligations of the Corporation."

This document was signed by

C. W. Chapin, Geo. A. Shaw,
Josiah Stickney, S. Johnson,
Jona. Bourne, Jr., Moses Kimball,
Ignatius Sargent, } *Directors.*

This was on the 2nd of January, 1867. On the 15th of January, 1868, a report is made to the shareholders containing these words, (the italics are my own,) "*It was the intention of the Directors from the first, to issue to the Stockholders at an early day, the unrestricted twenty thousand shares.*"

This last report was signed by every Director who signed the report in 1867, *with the exception of* Moses Kimball *and* Jona. Bourne Jr.!

The "early day" was five days after the adjournment of the Legislature, until which time "the intention of the Directors from the first," was kept a profound secret.

The judgment of the Legislature on this transaction was clearly expressed by the subsequent passage of an act,—

1868, Chap. 310.

Sect. 1. No railroad corporation, telegraph or gas-light company, chartered under the laws of this Commonwealth, shall hereafter declare any stock dividend, or divide the proceeds of the sale of stock among its stockholders, nor shall such corporation create any additional new stock, or issue certificates thereof to any person whatever, unless the par value of the shares so issued, is first paid in cash to the treasurer of said corporation.

Sect. 2. All certificates of stock issued in violation of the provisions of this act, shall be void; and the directors of any such corporation issuing the same shall be liable to a penalty of one thousand dollars each, to the use of the Commonwealth, to be recovered by indictment in any county where any of said directors reside: *provided*, That if any such director shall prove that previous to such issue he filed his dissent in writing thereto, with the clerk of said corporation, or was absent, and at no time voted therefor, he shall not be liable for the same.

Sec. 3. All acts and parts of acts inconsistent with the provisions of this act, are hereby repealed.

It is some satisfaction to know that the people are to be protected from undue taxation effected by such operations in future. But the injury is not yet so far removed into the past, that we can forget to seek indemnity if it be attainable. Through power obtained from the Legislature, *ostensibly for the public service and benefit*, and diverted in a great measure to private gains, the business of the State is forever subjected to an unnecessary burthen of $200,000 per annum. Is there any escape from the evil?

The Legislature might, under their power to "alter, amend and repeal" the charter, suspend or limit the dividends on the stock, until this sum, $2,000,000, and all dividends declared on the twenty thousand shares are paid into the treasury of the corporation, to be applied to the object for which the sum was asked by the directors, and granted by the State, to "complete and equip their road." It might be said, however, that this course, though just to the public, might be hard upon the shareholders of the Boston and Worcester, who received only ten per cent. on their stock, as an offset to this gift of $2,800,000 to the shareholders of the Western, depriving the former of an income to which they might think their claim was undoubted. I would suggest another means of relief to which no similar objection can be made.

The purchase of lands on deep water, and other expenses connected with the full developement of their business, will require additions to the capital of the road, of probably from four to six millions. The Treasurer of the Commonwealth informs me that the issue of $2,000,000, payable in twenty years, which was granted by the last Legislature, has not been sold, but that a loan has been effected on it of the Barings at five per cent. It is said that it is the intention of some of the directors, at a convenient season, to issue stock to the amount of two millions, to pay for the same, and return the scrip to the State. The result of this measure would be to give the shareholders the premium on the stock, amounting probably to $1,000,000, and oblige the citizens to pay them ten per cent. forever, instead of five per cent. to the Barings. The premium on this six or eight millions of stock, would amount probably to from three to four millions, which will find its way, under the present law, to the pockets of the shareholders.

When the State makes a grant of additional capital, it is simply an authority to tax the people ten per cent. on the amount. Such grants are supposed to be made solely for the public good and not with the idea of even collateral benefit to the shareholders. Now should the Legislature pass a law that hereafter all stock issued to this corporation should be sold at public auction by the State Treasurer, the par value paid over to the Treasurer of the corporation, and the premium, if any, placed in the sinking fund; the amount of unauthorized issue would be returned to the State without infringing on any legal or equitable right of the shareholders. It may be suggested that if the shareholders are not to receive a bonus on the shares, the directors might be unwilling to make those additions to their facilities which the public interest demands. I cannot, for a moment, anticipate such a result, but should it occur, the State would undoubtedly purchase the road and put it into the hands of those who would make the public good their first object.

This road was built by the people for the people, there was not a subscriber who ever expected to receive a cent for his money except in the benefit he derived, as a citizen, from diminishing the cost of his living and increasing the facilities for his business, and what has been the result? A careful accountant gives these figures:

Excess of dividends over six per cent. on money paid in,	$2,541,542
Loss of dividends less than six per cent., ...	891,000
	$1,650,542
Add the stock dividend of 1867, ...	2,000,000
	$3,650,542
Add the premium on 87,251 shares, at $47, ...	4,100,797
	$7,751,339

That is to say, the original subscriber who sold on the day of the junction would have received his capital, six per cent. on his money from the day he paid it, and his proportion of over seven millions of dollars bonus.

And yet, when the capitalists, who bought that stock with its accumulated interest at less than par, were asked, at a regular stockholders meeting, to lend, under the authority of the State, on ample security, the credit of the Corporation to enlarge its business and promote the prosperity of the State, and the city, the patriotism of whose citizens originated and carried it through, they were in fact told, that the Corporation owed nothing to the public, that it was simply a savings bank for widows.

Perhaps no stronger illustration can be given of the vast effects produced by supply and demand than one that is familiar to you all. Thousands of years ago, a monopoly, or what would now be called a corner in grain, was effected which gave to one man the entire control of the market. Its result, at the time, was to deprive a nation of all their property, and to reduce them to abject slavery. Its ultimate result, in the Providence of God, was to change the history of the world, and to influence the religious feeling and sentiment of mankind to the latest period. I allude, of course, to the famine in the time of

PHARAOH. By what is represented to be supernatural information, a young Hebrew knew that there were to be seven years of plenty, followed by seven years famine. He acted not on a calculation, but on a certainty. Having the confidence of the Monarch, and the command of the wealth of the nation, he built store cities, and laid up all the surplus production of the years of plenty. The famine came, and he held the key of the granaries,— and how did he use his power?— very much as the getter up of corners do at the present day. He exacted all that could be exacted without defeating his object, by the ruin of his customers. He first gathered up all the money that could be found in the land of Egypt and Canaan,— then he demanded and received all their cattle,—and when these were exhausted, bought all their land for PHARAOH, and then made the people slaves, and removed them from one part of the land to the other.

We rejoice that we live in a republic, and at a time when the modern facilities of intercourse render it out of the power of any individuals to obtain such a control over the absolute necessaries of life, as that obtained by the representative of King PHARAOH.

Let us look at our situation,— our demand in Massachusetts is certain; our supply depends not only on the fertility of the season, but on the means of transportation. It has been said that all the wheat raised in Massachusetts would not size her cotton cloth, and all the Indian corn would not feed her pigs and chickens.

We have a granary that would throw those of Egypt into the shade, and cattle upon unbounded prairies,— but they both lie at the distance of a thousand miles.

Who controls the gate of those prairies?

Who holds the key of that granary?

A dozen or more Presidents and Managers of the railroads between us and the food required by our daily necessities.

Should the daily welfare of a whole community depend on the disinterested virtue of these men, or of any other private individuals?

I have shown at what low rates transportation can be effected. I have shown what a difference would be made, if Directors were forbidden to make dividends on the millions of stock on which not a cent has been paid by the shareholders.

How then shall we reduce the cost of the necessaries of life?

My answer is, at once forbid any dividends to be paid on unpaid stock. And after that, take the keys of your granaries from the hands of those whose interest is only in increasing the gains of a small class, and place them in the hands of the representatives of the people.

www.ingramcontent.com/pod-product-compliance
Lightning Source LLC
LaVergne TN
LVHW020635110826
845149LV00004B/1197

9781418191108